53 PIANO SOLOS in the Early Grades

ED-1761

ISBN 978-0-7935-4993-1

G. SCHIRMER, Inc.

DISTRIBUTED BY

HAL•LEONARD®
CORPORATION

7777 W. BLUEMOUND RD. P.O. BOX 13819 MILWAUKEE, WI 53213

CONTENTS

See page 112 for Index by Composers

The Star-Spangled Banner

John Stafford Smith
Arranged by Margaret Bush

Con spirito

Piano

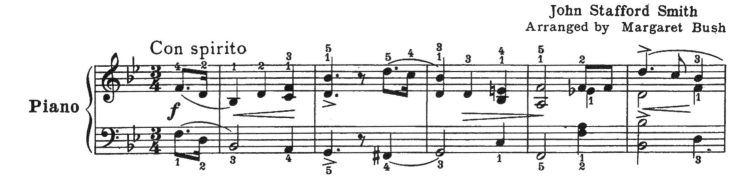

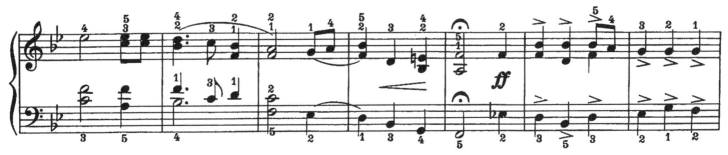

40172 x

My First Waltz

Bjarne Rolseth, Op. 40, No. 1

In modo di Valzer

Piano

mp sostenuto

40172

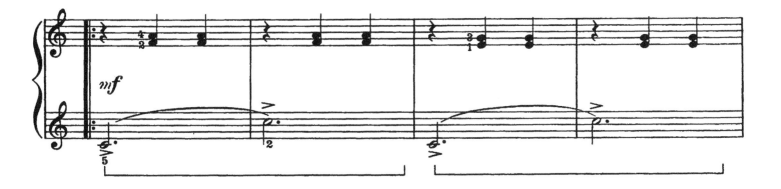

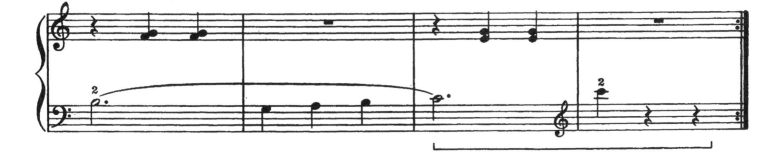

To Anne McPhail

Little Chief Red Feather

Elisabeth L. Hopson

Kitty-Kat Kapers

Fanny G. Eckhardt

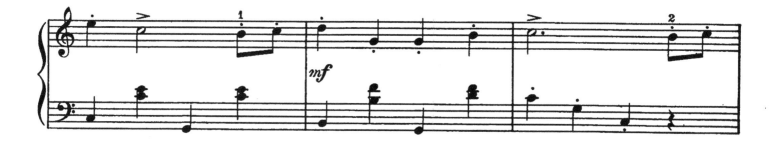

The Jolly Three

May Beth Ferguson

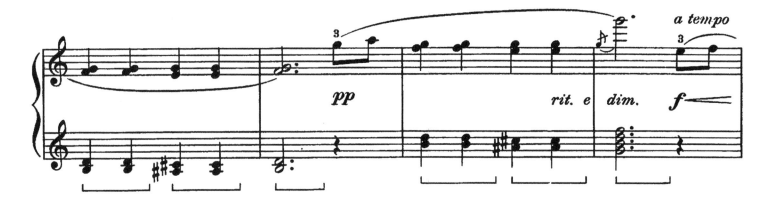

a tempo — Andante

rit.

espressivo

Tempo I⁰

f

più mosso

sfz

40172

To Mrs. A. C. Harrod

Down in the Cane Patch

Cora Mae Raezer

Brightly

The Puppet-Show

Martha Beck

40172

Sing a Song, Sailor

C. Franz Koehler

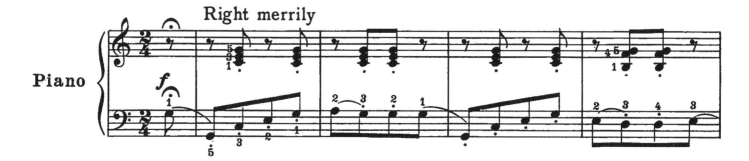

Little Fairy Waltz

Edited and fingered by
Maurice Gould

L. Streabbog. Op. 105, No. 1

Piano

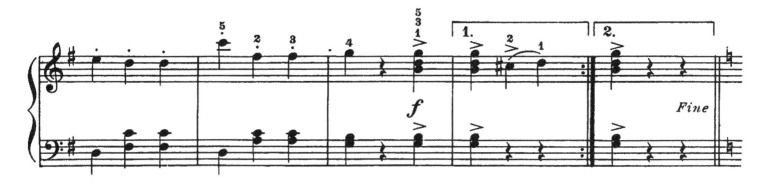

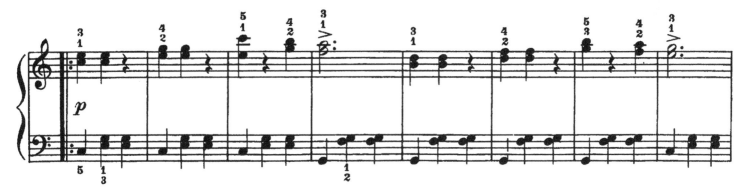

D. C.

The Merrymakers

Isabel Van Nort

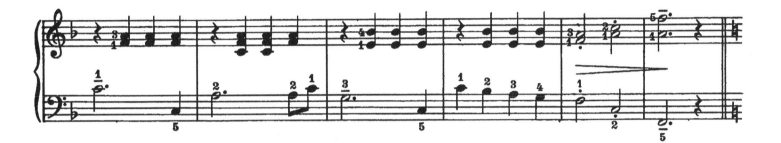

The Little Drum-Major

John J. Thomas

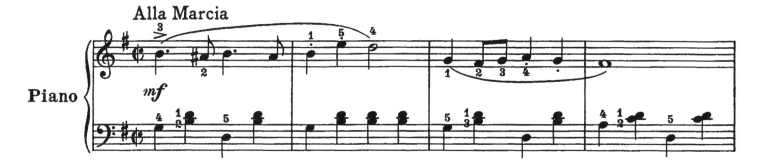

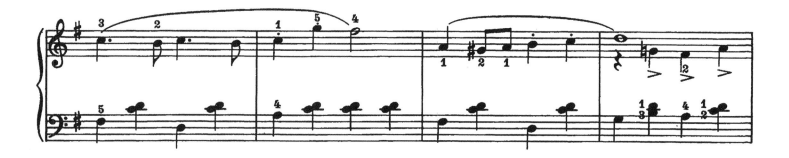

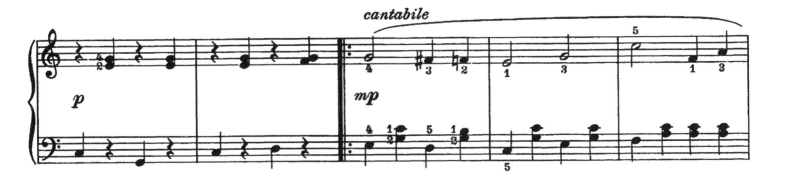

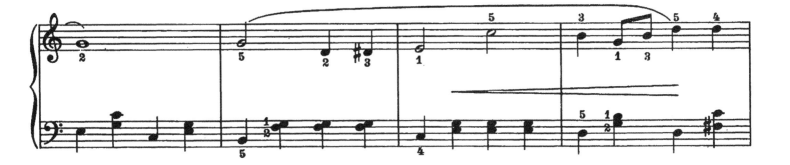

Dixie

Daniel D. Emmett
Arranged by Margaret Bush

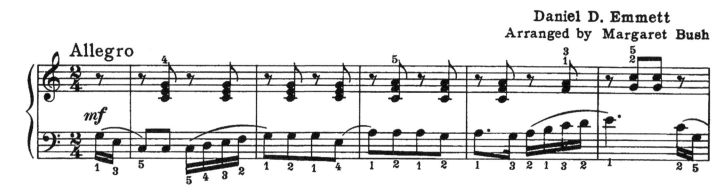

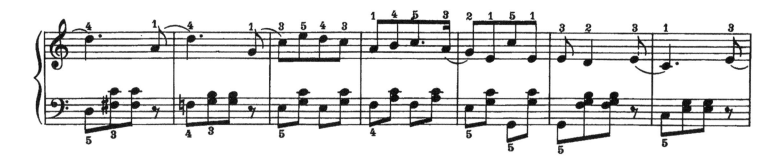

The Wild Horseman

Robert Schumann, Op.68, № 8

Allegro con brio. (♩. = 120)

To Helen Varina Simmons

Red Balloons

Grace L. Wright

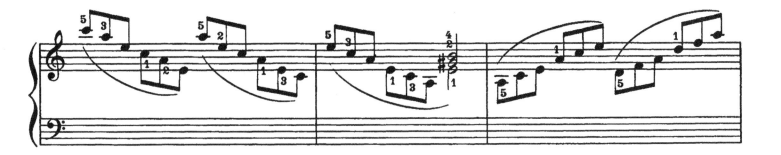

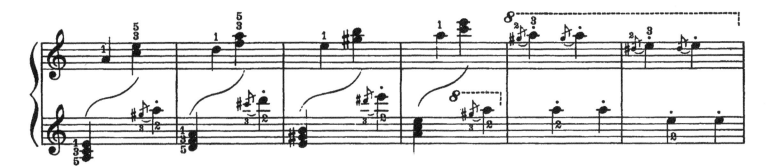

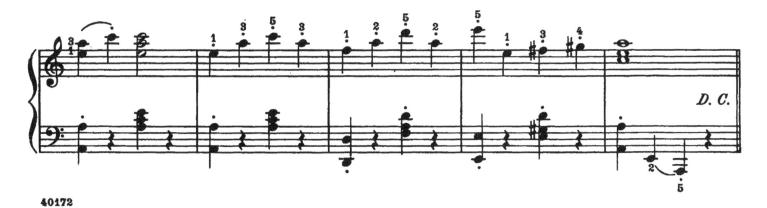

To Anne Brooke

Springtime Caprice

Helen Boykin

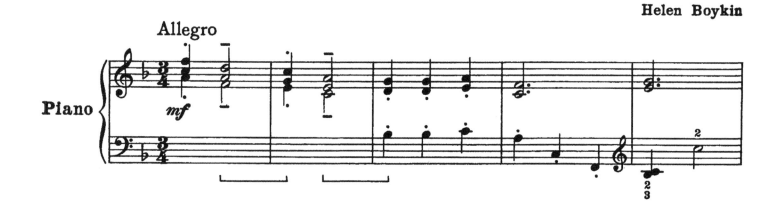
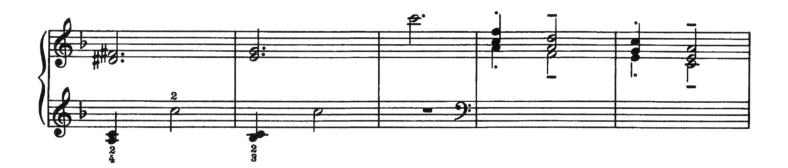

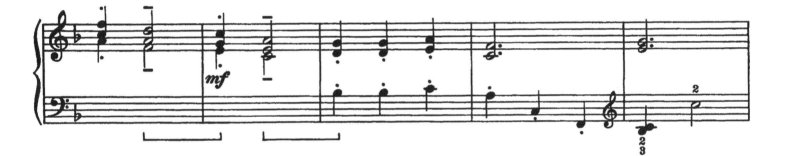

To Opal Louise Hayes

The Little Rag Dog

Bill Gillock

Playful, but not too fast

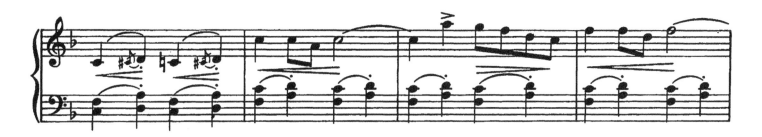

Minuet

from the Clavier Book of Anna Magdalena Bach

Edited by Walter Carroll

J. S. BACH

Animato (♩.= 69)

The Merry Farmer

Robert Schumann, Op. 68, No. 10

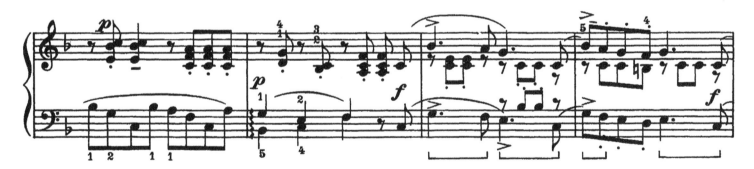

A Procession in Brittany

Josephine Bowden

40172

A Tropic Island

Bill Gillock

Smooth, not too slow

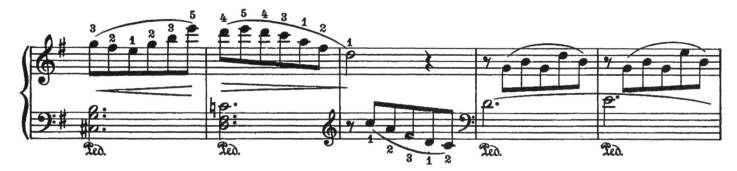

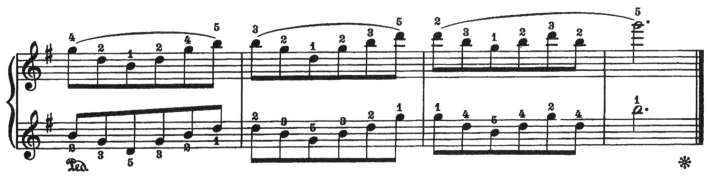

40172

Playing Soldiers
Jeu aux soldats

Edited by Carl Deis

Vladimir I. Rebikov
Op. 31, No. 4

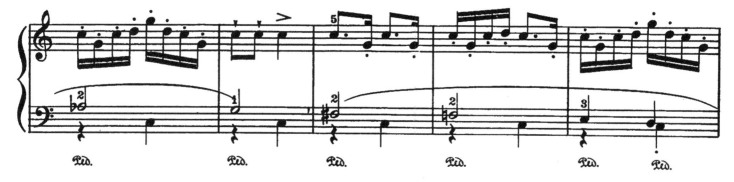

The Lame Witch Lurking in the Forest
La sorcière boiteuse rôdant par la forêt

Edited by Carl Deis

Vladimir I. Rebikov
Op. 31, No. 9

* To avoid use of pedal this figure should be played thus: etc., throughout the piece.

Indian War-Dance

BJARNE ROLSETH
Op. 38, No. 1

ed accel.   *f con fuoco*

mf

dim.   *p*

perdendosi   *pp*

40172

To Jeannine Dennis

Harmonica Rogue

C. Franz Koehler

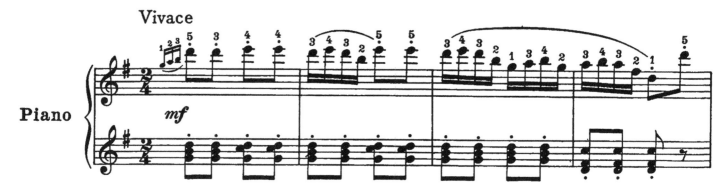

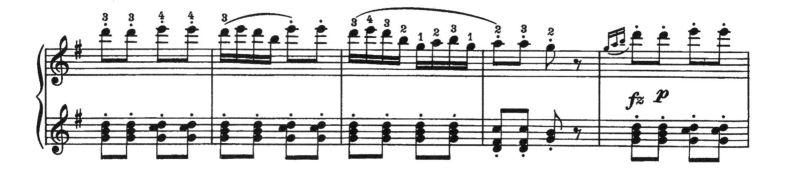

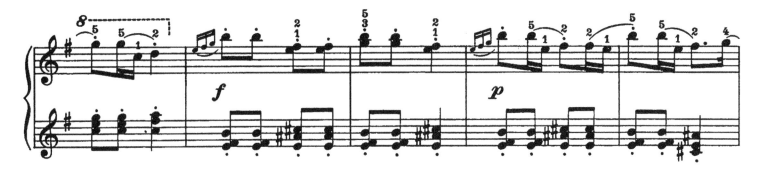

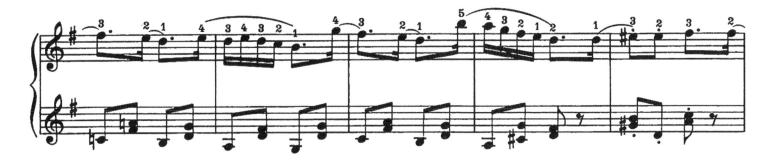

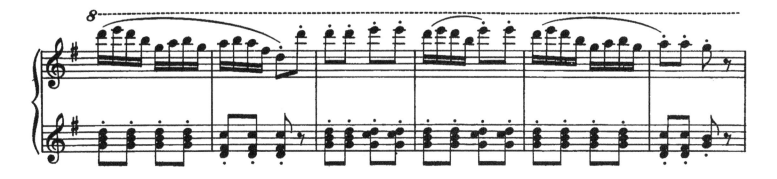

40172

Señorita

Tango

Lewis Brown

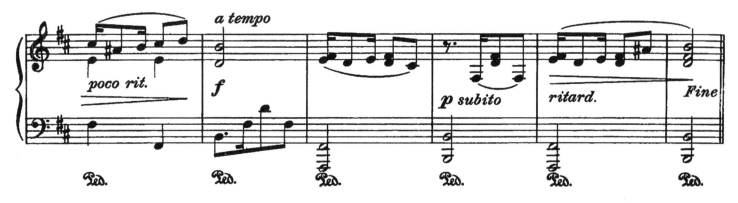

40172

Theme from

Sonata III

[K. 545]

Edited by
Richard Epstein
Abridged by C. D.

Wolfgang Amadeus Mozart

Allegro ♩ = 132

Piano

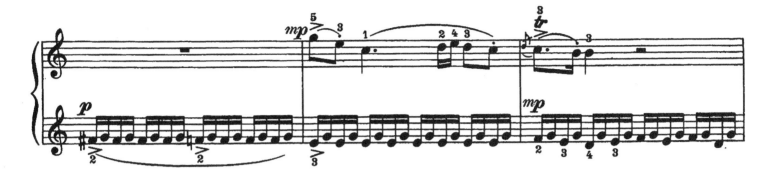

SONATINA.

Op. 36, Nº 2.

Muzio Clementi

Allegretto.

Allegro.

Minuet in G

Edited and fingered by
Carl Deis

Ludwig van Beethoven

40172

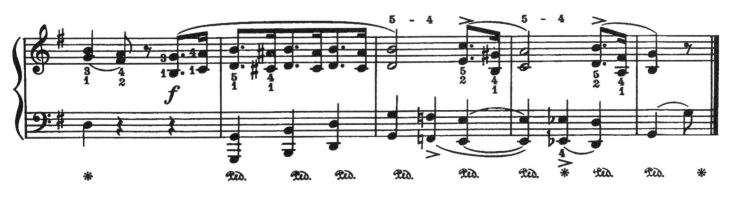

Minuet

(From the Opera "Don Giovanni")

W. A. Mozart

Entr'acte

From the Opera "Rosamunde"

F. Schubert

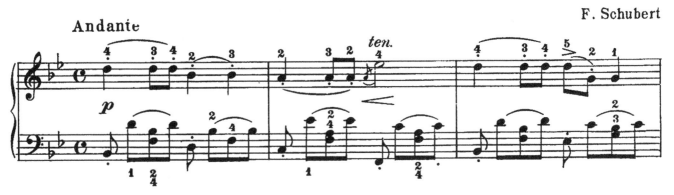

Bagatelle

Allegretto. (♩. = 84)

Ludwig van Beethoven, Op. 33, No. 8

Blue Danube Waltz

Edited by Carl Deis

Johann Strauss
Arranged by L. Streabbog, Op. 86

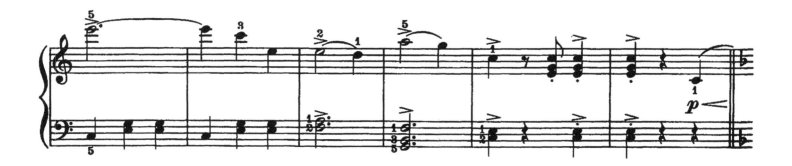

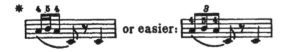 or easier:

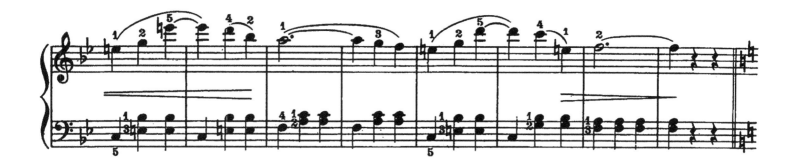

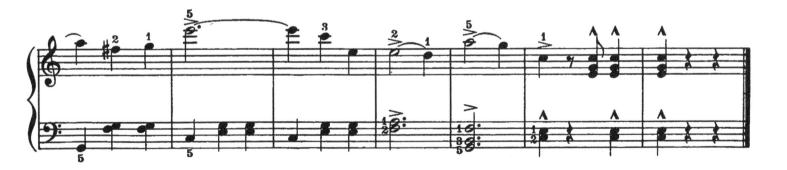

Petite Tarentelle

Stephen Heller. Op. 46, No.7

Largo

G. F. Händel

Molto sostenuto (♩=108)

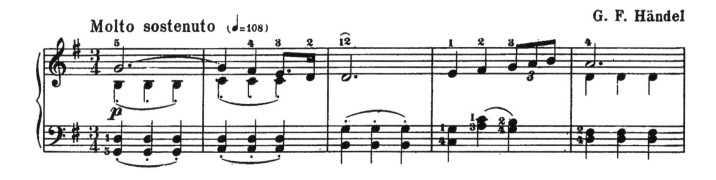

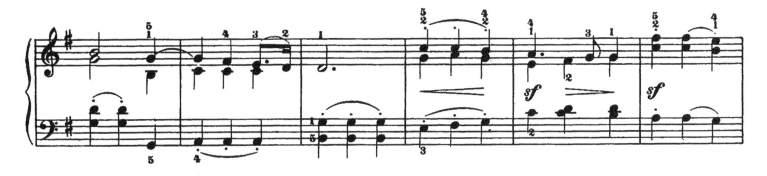

Courante.

Edited by G. Buonamici

George Frideric Handel

Solfeggio*
Étude

Edited and fingered by
Louis Oesterle

K. Ph. Em. Bach
(1714 – 1788)

Non troppo vivo

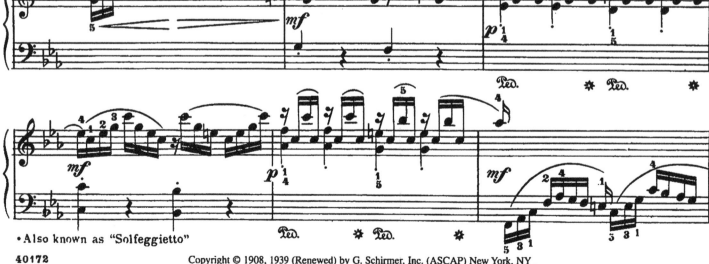

• Also known as "Solfeggietto"

(a) ♩ ♪ (b) According to some editions, the piece may end on the third beat.

40172

Prelude, Op. 28, No. 7

Simplified arrangement by
Carl Deis

Frédéric Chopin

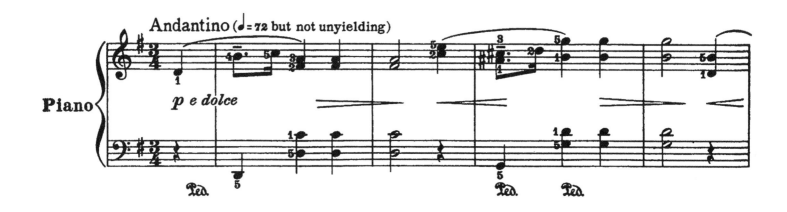

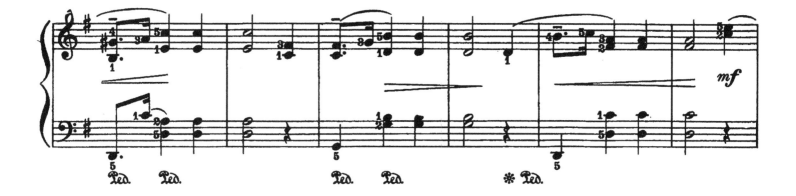

Prelude, Op. 28, No. 20

Simplified arrangement by
Carl Deis

Frédéric Chopin

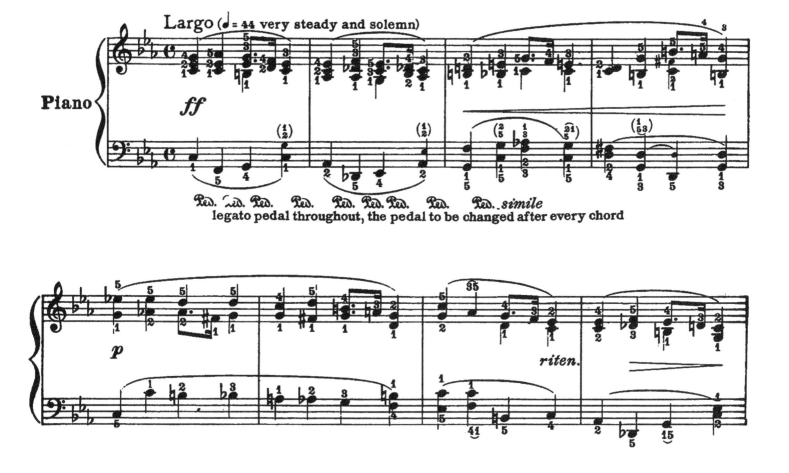

legato pedal throughout, the pedal to be changed after every chord

For M. B. H. R.

Cradle-Song
Wiegenlied

Johannes Brahms, Op. 49, No. 4
Arranged by Carl Deis

Dolce, con moto
Zart bewegt

Piano

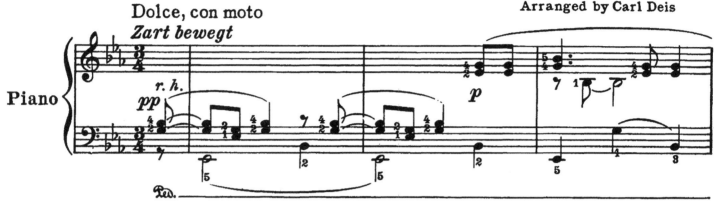

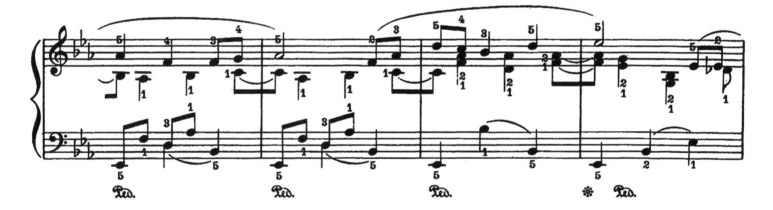
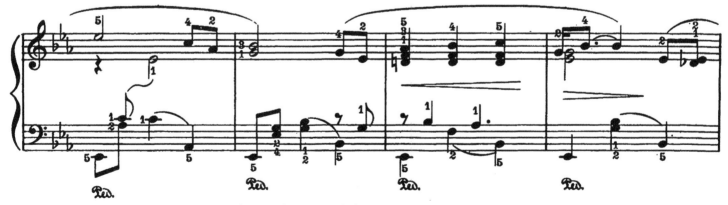

Spinning Song
(Spinnliedchen)

Edited and fingered by
Wm Scharfenberg.

ALBERT ELLMENREICH. Op.14, Nº4.

Grandmother's Minuet

Edited and fingered by
Louis Oesterle.

Edvard Grieg
Op. 68, N⁰ 2.

Allegretto grazioso e leggierissimo.

poco rit.

40172

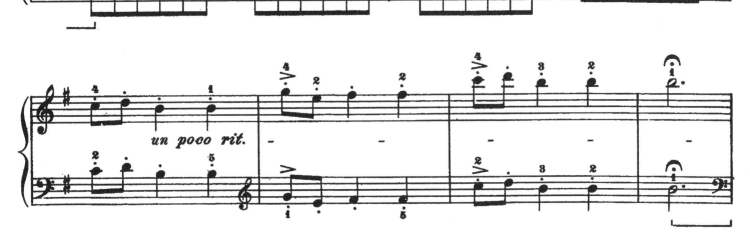

40172

Tempo I°

Ped. come sopra

Con moto

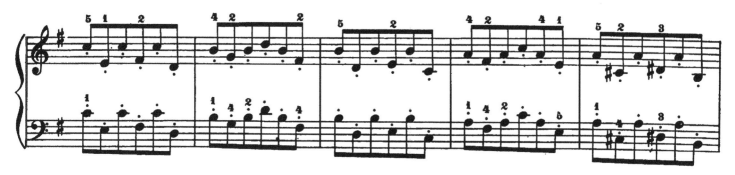

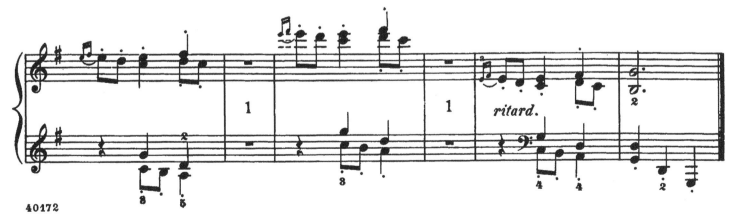

The Mill

I see a mill-wheel turning,
Through the alder trees;
Its singing and its roaring
Come rustling on the breeze.
Ah, welcome, welcome,
Sweet mill-wheel's song!
(Wilhelm Müller. Translation by W. W.)

Adolf Jensen

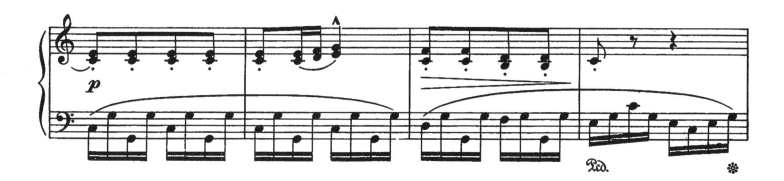

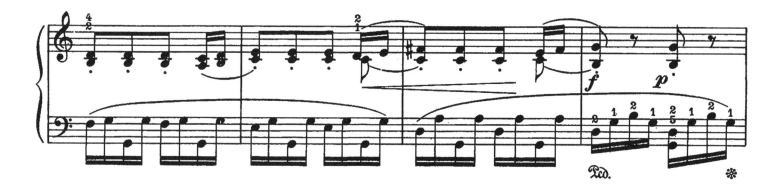

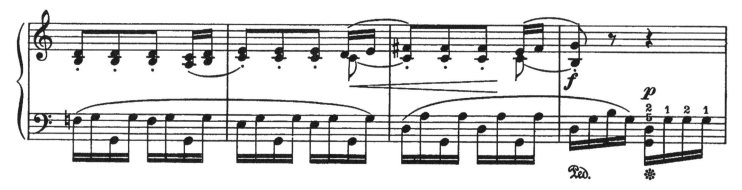

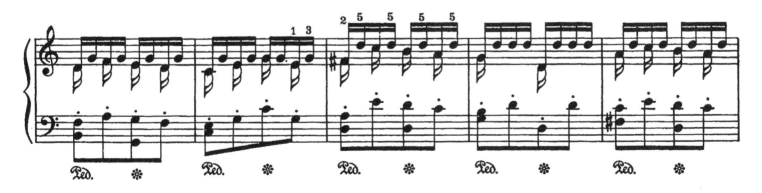

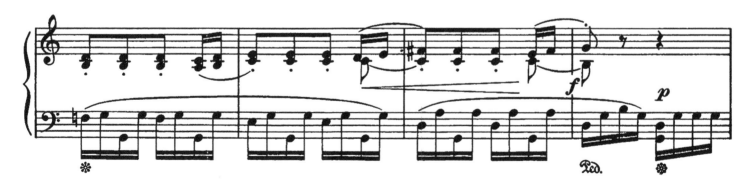

Purple Lupine

Arthur Farwell, Op. 86

With simplicity ♩ = 84

Piano

accel. slightly

retard   in time

3

ret.

40172

Intermezzo sinfonico

from the Opera

Cavalleria rusticana

Simplified Edition

P. Mascagni,
arr. by Max Spicker

Andante sostenuto

Piano

Élégie

Mélodie

from incidental music to Leconte de Lisle's drama "Les Érinnyes"

Jules Massenet, Op. 10, No.5
Arranged by Carl Deis

Lento e con gran sentimento

Piano

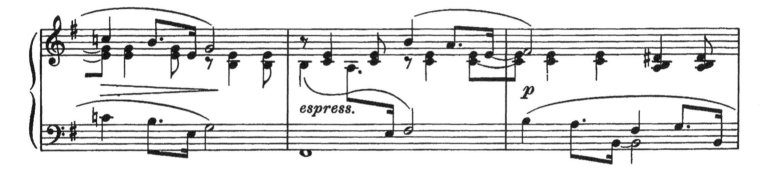

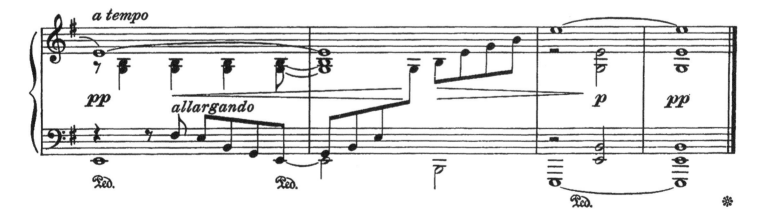

Sadness of Soul

F. Mendelssohn-Bartholdy. Op. 53, No. 4

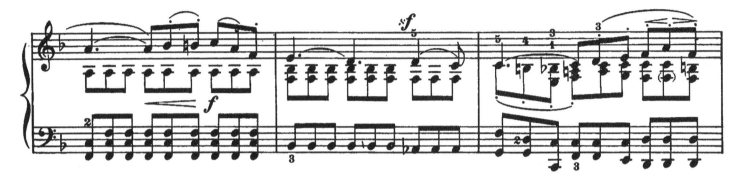

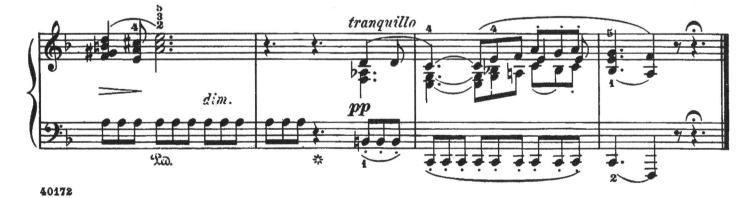

Sonata

Edited by Louis Oesterle

Domenico Scarlatti

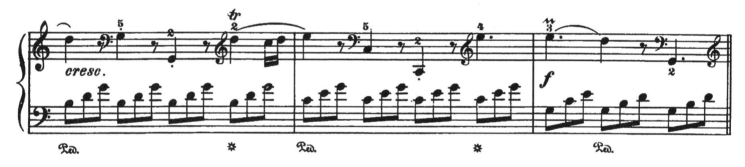

40172

THREE WALTZES.

Revised and fingered by
Wm Scharfenberg.

FR. SCHUBERT.

No 1.

Piano.

No 2.

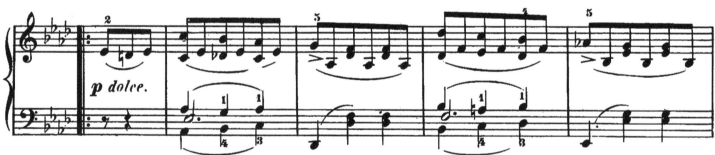

Nº 3.

Sweet Dreams

P. I. Tchaikovsky, Op. 39, No. 21

Berceuse from "Jocelyn"

by

B. GODARD

Edited and fingered by
LOUIS OESTERLE

Transcribed by
Alfred Kleinpaul

Recit.

"Ca - chés dans cet a - sile où Dieu nous a con - duits."
"Con - cealed in this re - treat where - to we have been led."

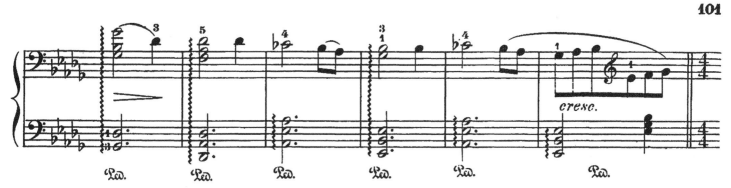

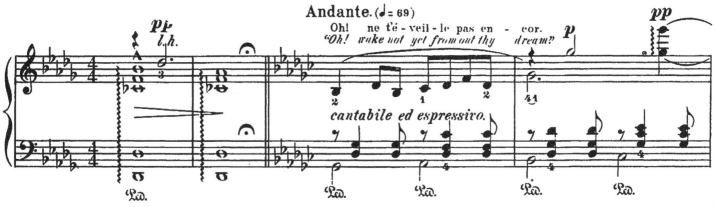

Andante. (♩ = 69)

Oh! ne t'é - veil - le pas en - cor.
"Oh! wake not yet from out thy dream?"

cantabile ed espressivo.

il canto marcato.

tranquillo.

40172

Andantino.

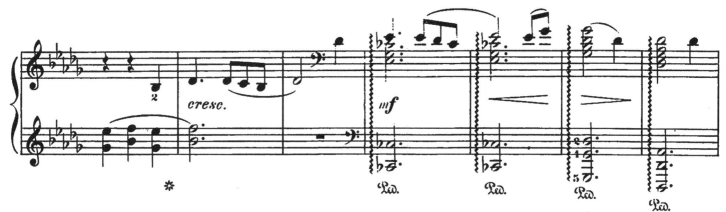

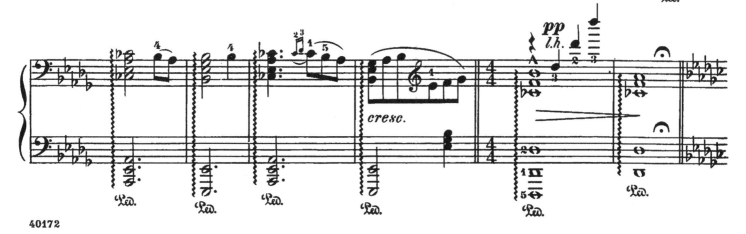

Dance of the Gnomes

Edited and fingered by
Louis Oesterle

E. Poldini

40172

Valse Viennoise

N. Louise Wright

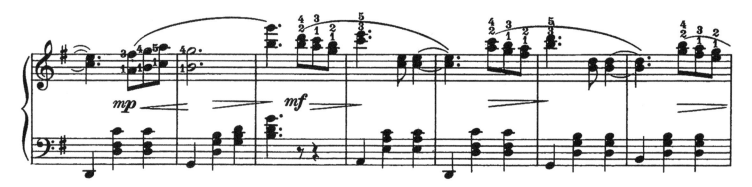

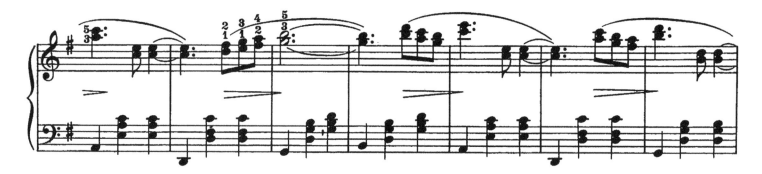

Butterflies

Edited and fingered by
Louis Oesterle

W. Lege. Op. 59, № 2

40172

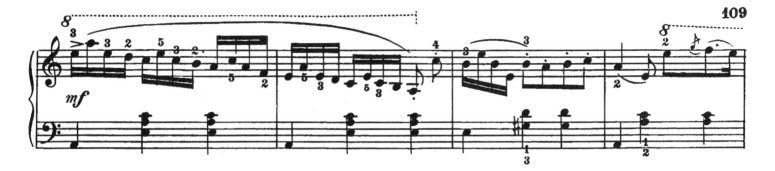

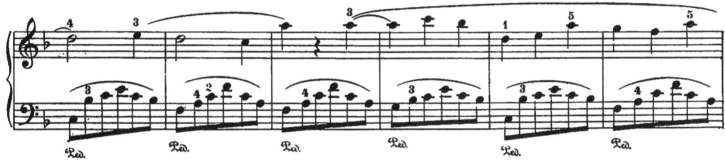

40172

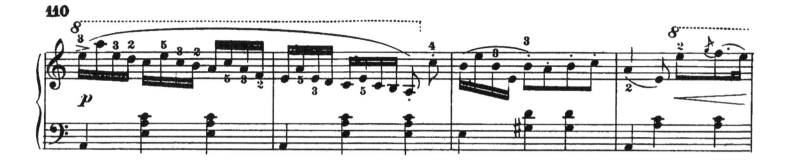

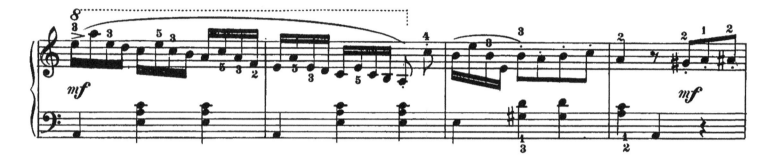

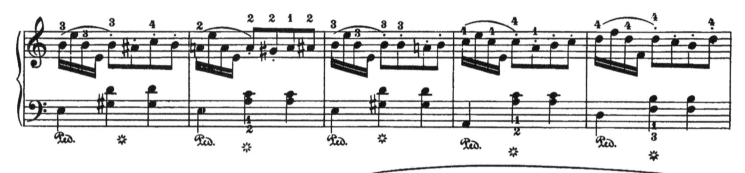

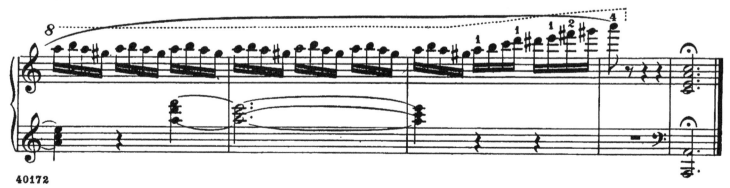

Album-Leaf
Albumblatt

Revised and fingered by W.S.

Edvard Grieg
Op. 12 No 7.

Allegretto

Piano

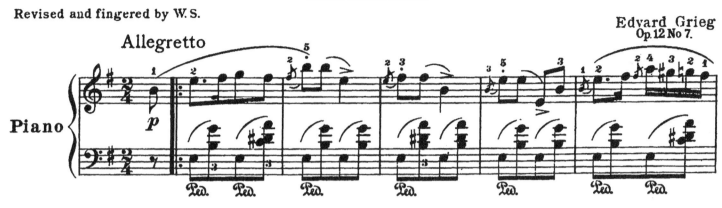

40172

ALPHABETICAL INDEX BY COMPOSERS